Embrace Your Shadow to Find Your Light

Also by Nancy Levin

NANCY LEVIN

Embrace Your Shadow to Find Your Light

A Shadow Work Journal

HAY HOUSE LLC

Carlsbad, California • New York City
London • Sydney • New Delhi

Tradepaper ISBN: 978-1-4019-7893-8

10 9 8 7 6 5 4 3 2 1
1st edition, June 2024

Printed in the United States of America

This product uses responsibly sourced papers and/or recycled materials. For more information, see www.hayhouse.com.

Contents

Introduction

In times of inner and outer turmoil, illuminating your shadow can be an essential tool for self-reflection. As the title of this journal demonstrates, the willingness to dive into your shadow is one of the most powerful ways you can embrace all parts of yourself, including and especially the ones you've disowned, repressed, and learned to compartmentalize—because these are the very places w here your purpose and brilliance hide.

I was personally trained by my late friend and mentor Debbie Ford, who is credited with bringing the concept of shadow work to a mass audience through her appearances on *The Oprah Winfrey Show* and *Super Soul Sunday*. The best-selling author of several books, including *The Dark Side of the Light Chasers*, Debbie was an internationally recognized coach, speaker, and teacher who revolutionized the term *shadow work*. Debbie's purpose was to help people understand and claim their shadow aspects. My work has a foundation in hers, and she was a big part of my impetus to start Levin Life Coach Academy in 2019, especially since Debbie had personally selected me to carry on her legacy.

In honoring that legacy, *Embrace Your Shadow to Find Your Light: A Shadow Work Journal* is my gift to you.

What Is the Shadow?

Whether your shadow stretches behind you as you face the sunrise or flickers along beside you as you rush down a hallway in the night, it's always there. In the same way, the shadow part of yourself—those aspects of you that you've forgotten or tucked away in the darkness of your inner world—is always there.

The term shadow, in this context, was first coined by Swiss psychoanalyst Carl Gustav Jung. In the 1968 book, *Collected Works of C.G. Jung, Volume 9 (Part 1): Archetypes and the Collective Unconscious*, he says:

> The shadow is that hidden, repressed, for the most part inferior and guilt-laden personality whose ultimate ramifications reach back into the realm of our animal ancestors. . . . If it has been believed hitherto that the human shadow was the source of evil, it can now be ascertained on closer investigation that the unconscious man, that is his shadow, does not consist only of morally reprehensible tendencies, but also displays a number of good qualities, such as normal instincts, appropriate reactions, realistic insights, creative impulses, etc.

Although parts of Jung's definition are useful, Debbie Ford developed a definition of the shadow that fits our more modern understanding of human nature:

Our shadow is made up of all the parts of ourselves that we hide, deny, suppress, and don't see in ourselves—both the positive and the negative. Our shadow is all the aspects that we reject out of shame, fear, or disapproval.

However you wish to describe it, there's a time in everyone's life when you come face-to-face with your shadow. The invitation is to integrate it and gently cast light on your hidden truths. These include your closeted fears, unresolved emotions, and suppressed desires. As both Jung and Ford understood, and as this journal will reveal to you, the aspect of self you call your shadow is the part of you that holds your power—but only when you are willing to explore its hidden depths.

In fact, willingly descending into the cave of your shadow incrementally enhances your relationship with yourself—by improving self-trust, self-love, and self-acceptance as you explore the depths of your psyche that contain your buried treasure.

Here are some further distinctions to help you understand exactly what your shadow is, as well as what it isn't.

What It Is

- Something we all have
- Something that is misunderstood
- Something that remains hidden and unknown—until it pops up unexpectedly in your thoughts, words, emotions, and behaviors, often causing you

to go, "Wow, I have no idea why I thought/felt/said/did that!"

- Something that can be explored through creativity, dreams, meditation, journaling, etc., as it often lives in the language of symbols

- Something you've either rejected or denied (includes attributes you deny in yourself or others—such as rage, laziness, cowardice, egotism—or positive attributes you don't think you have and consequently idealize in others—such as courage, motivation, sensuality, empathy), usually out of fear sourced in past experiences

- Something that often gets projected onto the outside world: onto individuals, groups, etc., to other those whom you perceive as different from you, and to further separate you from both yourself and others

- A source that, once understood, comes bearing gifts and can lead to positive growth

What It Isn't

- Bad
- Evil
- Something that'll ruin your life if you engage with it
- Something that only exists in other people, places, or situations

- Completely knowable, since it lives in the unconscious mind, which is more or less infinite

We tend to be hung up on labels, but getting to know your shadow helps you embrace both the nuances of the world as it is and your own inner world—it's not either/or; it's both/and. Even in some spiritual and personal development work, we are often urged to walk away from our so-called darkness and toward our light. The truth is, your light and darkness are two sides of the same coin. If you only accept one over the other, you ignore your essential complexity, beauty, and depth—and ultimately, you pay the price.

Integrating your shadow is a process that mirrors the phases of the moon. You see the moon in different phases throughout the month, from new to full and new again. When it's fully illuminated by the sun, it appears as a perfect round ball. But when the moon is waxing or waning, you only see parts of it, while other parts remain immersed in darkness. However, the moon is always whole, no matter what you do or don't see. It is simply revealing or concealing parts of itself at different times. All of us do the same thing: We spend a good chunk of our lives concealing parts of ourselves we don't want to be and don't want others to see. But no matter what, we are still whole, made up of shadow and light.

Once you recognize you have access to *everything*, every quality and experience and state of being, you stop hiding and are no longer afraid to express all of who you are. And when you reflect and embody your wholeness, you encourage others to do the same.

What Is Shadow Work?

Shadow work is a tool for returning to wholeness and integrating all parts of the self—the parts we identify with strongly, as well as those we push away or deny—through a methodical process of self-inquiry and discovery that leads to healing.

Shadow work helps you to be very discerning about the parts of your life you've been estranged from, usually because of fear, and encompasses everything from meditation to journaling to somatic exercises. *Somatic* means "directly related to the body," helping you bypass the conscious mind and activate the unconscious, which can lead to deeper healing. These techniques can include breath work, dance, yoga, activating the voice, and increasing interoception—or the sense that helps you figure out how you feel inside your body. Altogether, they open your mind to what has remained concealed or repressed.

When you begin this deep excavation work, you start to witness and capture the entirety of your essence, which is beautiful beyond words. Although shadow work isn't easy, as it will surely ask you to dredge up painful memories or experiences and thoughts that surface fear or shame, doing this inner work will help you claim all of who you are with love rather than judgment. In fact, although shadow work may hold ominous connotations, like walking around a dark landscape without a flashlight, it's not so scary when you approach it with an open mind and open heart. As you start to shine the light of your curiosity inward, you'll find valuable information about how you came to be who you are—and how you might choose different, healthier pathways of self-expression and connection to yourself and the world.

When certain experiences and qualities become a part of your shadow landscape, this is usually because you associate them with pain. But when you look upon your pain with the light of compassion and the willingness to apply healing care to the neglected terrain, you discover that all it wanted was your love and attention. You learn that interacting with your shadow from a place of curiosity rather than fear helps you regulate your emotions and change your perceptions of yourself and the world in ways that serve rather than hinder you.

Most of us have places in our life where we don't feel joyful, fulfilled, or complete, and those missing pieces can push us to seek external validation from others—sometimes through counting likes on social media or clinging to relationships we have long outgrown. Instead of trying to get your needs met by others, shadow work invites you to go deeper within yourself so that *you* can be the key to your own wholeness. And truly, the only way to experience wholeness is to ensure that all parts of you are attended to and working in harmony—because you are truly an amalgamation of all pairs of opposites, from light and darkness to feminine and masculine.

When you don't consciously and intentionally do shadow work, you may experience self-sabotage, depression, anxiety, and other disorders of the soul. Trying to escape from what pains you only worsens matters. Shadow work, and the journey you're about to embark on in this journal, guides you to understand and transmute your pain into wisdom and purpose.

Debbie Ford had a term that she called the *beachball effect*. She said that you can certainly do your best to push down every thought, feeling, or behavior you've ever deemed unacceptable—but just like how a beach ball always pops up after it's been submerged in water, those thoughts, feelings, and behaviors you're shoving down will eventually blast up to the surface. When you do not tend your inner landscape by paying attention to your emotions, you risk an explosion of your shadow qualities. Often, when you least want or expect it, some part of you that's been rejected pops up and destroys the illusion of your fixed and stable life.

We tend to expend a lot of energy holding our shadow parts down, suppressing them within our psyche. Shadow work is an act of radical honesty—of facing yourself in the mirror and claiming what is true, even if it causes you discomfort. The amazing thing about this simple act is that it begins to melt away the armor you've built around yourself so you can see and access the light within . . . which is waiting to bathe you in its healing warmth.

The Benefits of Shadow Work

There are so many benefits to doing shadow work, but for the purpose of this journal, here are the main ones:

- Greater emotional intelligence
- A stronger connection to yourself, including the parts of you that remain under wraps
- A clearer, deeper relationship with your intuition and the reservoir of creativity that lives within
- A greater awareness of your patterns and behaviors (especially the fear-based, self-sabotaging ones) that ensure you are no longer unconsciously controlled by them

- A greater awareness of the deeper needs and desires of your heart and soul and how you can meet them

- A sense of overall inner harmony and well-being that comes when your inner parts are no longer in conflict

- A life that is powered by wisdom and compassion rather than fear and avoidance

- More intimate, honest relationships—with yourself and everyone around you

- A connection to all beings that is mirrored by your experience of the wholeness you feel within yourself

The Magic and Metaphor of Alchemy

Throughout this journal, the metaphor of alchemy will be used to guide you through your shadow work. Alchemy was the medieval predecessor of chemistry. Alchemists did everything from making medicines and metallic alloys to crafting perfumes and cosmetics. For the most part, they were invested in understanding and isolating the building blocks of nature and matter.

Alchemy was founded on the idea that matter is made up of four elements: earth, air, fire, and water. It was believed that, depending on the combination of these elements, you could produce powerful transformations, from curing diseases to fashioning beautiful tools. By the same token, these elements in the wrong balance could create disease or generate conflict.

At its deepest and most secretive, alchemists were interested in transmuting base metal into gold and discovering material means for mystical ends. The most famous pursuit of alchemists was finding a universal elixir known as the philosopher's stone, a perfectly balanced substance that was said to have the power not only to transform metals into gold, but to grant eternal youth and life to whoever used it. Jung, who explored alchemy in his own work, felt it was the key to wholeness:

> The purpose of Alchemy is to liberate the whole individual which is hidden in the darkness, threatened by the rational and correct conduct of life, consequently experiencing themselves as hindered and on the wrong path.

Was the philosopher's stone a tangible physical object or a metaphysical concept? We don't know for certain. It seems fitting that the language around it was so vague and obscure, as the journey to balance is highly subjective. As you do your own shadow work, consider it your personal initiation into the mystery of wholeness. Your underworld descent won't look like anyone else's, nor will your ascent into the light.

Although we don't know all the specifics, medieval alchemists had a process for converting base metals into gold, and of seeking that elusive philosopher's stone, that required seven distinct steps: calcination, dissolution, separation, conjunction, fermentation, distillation, and coagulation. For the purpose of this journal, the language of these steps has been updated. Each step holds true to the original alchemical stage it represents, but in this case, you're not literally trying to get from base metal to gold. Rather, shadow work is a form of soul alchemy that helps you to find liberation and wholeness.

The steps you'll travel through are:

- **Awareness:** In this stage, you shine a light on the shadow, taking stock of what's there.

- **Surrender:** You let go of control and allow yourself to connect to the qualities of the shadow, free of judgment.

- **Responsibility:** This is the point where you learn from your shadow. You own what you've disowned and forgive yourself for any of the painful memories and emotions that come up.

- **Authenticity:** Here, you embody all you've learned. You also exercise radical honesty by sharing more of yourself.

- **Resilience:** Now it's time to test your authenticity in the real world, recognizing that you may continue to experience shame and the desire to hide out; however, you commit to moving in the direction of wholeness.

- **Nourishment:** This is where you readjust, adapt, and dip back into your shadow to discover new information and new ways to self-regulate as you harmonize your inner and outer worlds.

- **Wholeness:** You have come to familiarize yourself with more and more of your shadow, and the result is that you shine from within.

You reflect vulnerability and transparency as
you share your light and gifts with yourself
and the world.

Remember that while these may seem to be linear
steps, the shadow is like an onion—it has lots of layers,
and the more you're ready to see, the more those layers
start to peel off and reveal themselves. More and more
of what has been unconscious will become conscious as
you do your shadow work, but wholeness is a journey,
not a destination. You are an infinite being, and as such,
shadow work is something you'll hopefully continue to do
throughout your life so you can access more and more of
your luminosity.

How to Use This Journal

Each journal prompt, exercise, and meditation is
meant to be a stepping stone toward deeper self-awareness
and transformational healing as you witness and harness
the essence of your wholeness. This isn't the same as being
happy, but it is about experiencing deeper meaning, fulfillment, and satisfaction as you befriend the parts of yourself that have been hiding out in the darkness.

You'll start by identifying an issue you might be deal-
ing with—something that is calling out for your attention.
From this situation, you'll begin to identify shadow qualities you'd like to intentionally explore. A *shadow quality*
is a trait that's connected to any behavior we reject or disown in ourselves. Although it can take a bit of digging to
recognize your shadow qualities, you'll be guided to identify them by noticing things like uncomfortable feelings
and behaviors that trigger you. At the same time, a shadow

quality can be something that is undeniably positive but that you haven't accepted as part of your inner landscape. We all disown qualities we've defined as either good or bad, and the result is that they get trapped or hidden in our shadow. The more hidden they are from our awareness, the harder it is to experience fulfillment, because we've cut off a piece of our own wholeness, whether it's a piece we like or not.

As you learn to step into the shadow with willingness and curiosity, you incrementally develop a sense of trust and safety within yourself—even when you have no idea what you'll find.

You can choose to dive into the deep end with the issue you explore, but dipping your big toe in and going slowly at first, especially if you are new to this process, is often the best method. Shadow work can be very tender, so move at a pace that feels restorative while expanding your capacity to go deep.

Journaling is a powerful way to converse with ourselves—a true act of self-revelation—which is why it's an important aspect of this shadow work journey. However, it doesn't have to be a formal process you do at a special time with a particular pen and scented candle, unless the act of ritualizing the work to create a journaling practice is a goal for you.

Don't be afraid to get messy and raw. If you can't tell yourself the unvarnished truth, it will be impossible to do that elsewhere. You can respond to the prompts any way you'd like: through freewriting, poetry, drawing, collage, or even fragmented, incomplete thoughts you write down in bullet points. Feel free to throw out the rules of grammar and syntax. As long as you are committed to showing up fully present, there is no wrong way to do any of this.

Beyond the journaling prompts, there are integration exercises and short meditations that will help you experience how liberating it is to be with all parts of yourself versus expending energy on keeping them tucked away. As you continue through this process, you will learn to become a more agile soul spelunker, and you'll gradually build your confidence when it comes to descending into your depths and unlocking hidden doors to discover the treasure within.

If you're ready to find true north in the darkness, grab your headlamp, and let's go!

STAGE 1:
AWARENESS

Alchemical Stage—CALCINATION:

The process of heating a substance to a high temperature but below the melting or fusing point, causing loss of moisture, reduction or oxidation, and dissociation into simpler substances.

In shadow work, this is the process of starting to break down the ego and attachment to your worldly ideas.

✦ ✦ ✦

Stage 1 of your journey is **Awareness**. This is where you'll be shining a light on the shadow and taking stock of what's there. This is also where you'll gain an initial recognition of the parts of your shadow that are beckoning for your attention.

It's not possible to ever completely know one's shadow, since we are infinite beings, but there are ways you can start to observe it—namely, by noticing its effects in your life.

The TEACH Method

How can you start to make sense of what lives in the shadow? Before you begin digging around in the more subterranean regions, you can start to shine a light into the darkness in a variety of ways. TEACH is an acronym that spells out the reactions and tendencies you can learn to recognize as signals from your shadow. TEACH stands for the following:

- **Trigger:** Things that anger and irritate you about others
- **Enamor:** The qualities you idolize in others that you've disowned in yourself
- **Avoid:** The people, situations, and qualities you intentionally or unconsciously steer clear of
- **Criticize:** The attributes you strongly dislike in yourself and that you try to hide
- **Hold Back:** The often-transformative experiences and emotions you deprive yourself of

Each aspect of TEACH has a belief and an origin story that offers insight into how that belief was formed. Some examples are:

- **Trigger:** "Needy people are so pathetic and draining."
  Origin story: Maybe you feel this way because you were shamed for expressing your needs when you were a child, so you learned to take care of yourself—and it annoys you when you see that other people can express their needs so clearly compared to you.

- **Enamor:** "Artists are my favorite people—I wish I could be like them."
  Origin story: You loved to draw, write, and perform when you were a kid, but your third-grade teacher told you that you weren't

a good artist, so you stopped expressing yourself that way and instead admired creative people from afar.

- **Avoid:** "I feel sick when I'm around conflict and confrontation—it's best to avoid it at any cost." *Origin story:* You grew up in a chaotic family where people screamed to be heard. Ever since, you told yourself that you just don't need that kind of drama.

- **Criticize:** "I hate being lazy—it makes me feel like such a loser." *Origin story:* Your older sister was lazy, according to your family. Her life turned out to be messy, and she's currently in debt up to her ears. Your parents are constantly complaining about having to bail her out. You've sworn you'll never be like her.

- **Hold Back:** "I'm never going to let myself be vulnerable—others will take advantage of me." *Origin story:* You've had your heart broken in the past, and you've professed that you'll never let yourself take the emotional risk to feel that kind of pain again, even if it means never finding love.

As you start to notice these signals from your shadow, this process will bring up old stories/experiences and the subsequent shadow beliefs you formed about yourself. That awareness doesn't come automatically; after all, when you disown certain qualities, you usually have reasonable excuses for why this is so. But when you dig deeper, you'll recognize that the decision to disown usually came about because of an experience that taught you something about who you should or should not be.

Your limiting shadow beliefs hold immense power over your life, telling you what you can and cannot do, who you can or cannot be. But here's the thing, beliefs are just stories we tell ourselves about the way the world works, and our role within it. Your shadow beliefs were formed in reaction to the negative experiences you had in childhood that you were too young to understand, so you made these experiences mean something about you and drew a conclusion about yourself. Shadow beliefs sound like: I'm not good enough, I'm not enough, I'm unlovable, I'm unworthy, and the only thing holding these shadow beliefs in place is that you believe them.

Reclaiming What You've Disowned

When it comes down to it, we push away and disown certain qualities within us due to fear and shame, which are usually associated with experiences that brought us pain in the past. We learned to shut off these qualities in order to keep ourselves from feeling pain.

The unconscious mind is a genius—it takes in and processes everything the conscious mind is too busy or overwhelmed to feel. You don't have to love any of those characteristics that make you feel gnarly inside. But the awareness stage encourages you to remain curious and compassionate and to consider that maybe it's okay to feel that old pain, because now you have tools to transmute it—as well as the stories and shadow beliefs that formed in response to it.

You don't have to dig too deep to start getting signs of where your shadow lives. After all, when you focus on the negative parts of your disowned qualities, this usually means you'll attract and be triggered by people and situations that carry those same qualities. The more you disown greediness, the more you'll be irritated by greedy people around you—this is actually the unconscious mind's way of urging you to look inward instead of keeping your attention on the outside!

Often, the quality you *reject*, you tend to *project* onto others. The more you're in rejection mode, the more you'll tend to notice and attract people who openly act out that shadow quality. Ironically, they're actually giving you the opportunity to reclaim the quality you disowned—by holding up a mirror so you can start to see it in yourself.

Shadow work helps us to take back our projections and reclaim our wholeness. For example, when you acknowledge your own greediness and have compassion for this quality inside yourself—even though it may present differently than it does in other people—you stop being as triggered when it shows up in others.

It can be challenging to imagine owning and embracing parts of yourself you've judged as bad and wrong. But every part of you comes bearing gifts. Think about it: It may come in handy to be "greedy" at times, such as treating yourself to a well-deserved pleasure and enjoying your life in greater ways. "Needy" can be empowering and connecting if you're someone who's used to doing everything on your own.

By the same token, you can start to reframe the more exalted qualities you may be holding yourself back from, like vulnerability, joy, sensuality, etc. All of these have tremendous gifts connected to your self-expression and wholeness.

Ultimately, when you disown some aspect of yourself, you are usually judging it via harsh and severely limiting standards and perceptions. This encourages an either/or perspective—either you have a quality or you don't, it's either good or bad, etc. You may stuff down certain qualities in order to be loved and accepted, without getting curious about how these qualities can also be assets.

In suppressing these parts of who you are, you suppress your light. You might fail to take the risks that will lead to greater fulfillment and self-expression, like accessing creativity or getting vulnerable in love. The gift of awareness is that you are prompted to step into your wholeness and out of binary/dualistic thinking. And the more access you have to all parts of who you are, the more power you can claim for yourself.

On the following pages, you will follow the TEACH method in a series of journal prompts to identify your disowned shadow qualities.

JOURNAL PROMPTS

Cultivating Awareness

Trigger

What are the qualities I am most triggered by in others?

Choose a specific quality from your list that you feel intuitively called to explore and write it here.

What are some of the stories I have about this quality? (These can include recurring or powerful dreams, since the shadow shows up through the subconscious and symbols.)

What was my earliest experience with this quality?

What are some of the beliefs I formed as a result?

Enamor

What are the qualities I am most enamored of in others that I don't think I have?

Choose a specific quality from your list that you feel intuitively called to explore and write it here.

What are some of the stories I have about this quality?
(These can include recurring or powerful dreams, since the shadow shows up through the subconscious and symbols.)

What was my earliest experience with this quality?

What are some of the beliefs I formed as a result?

Avoid

What kinds of people, places, and situations do I avoid?

Choose a specific quality from your list that you feel intuitively called to explore and write it here.

What are some of the stories I have about this quality?
(These can include recurring or powerful dreams, since the
shadow shows up through the subconscious and symbols.)

What was my earliest experience with this quality?

What are some of the beliefs I formed as a result?

Criticize

What do I tend to be critical of in myself?

Choose a specific quality from your list that you feel intuitively called to explore and write it here.

What are some of the stories I have about this quality?
(These can include recurring or powerful dreams, since the shadow shows up through the subconscious and symbols.)

What was my earliest experience with this quality?

What are some of the beliefs I formed as a result?

Hold Back

What do I tend to hold back from feeling or experiencing?

Choose a specific quality from your list that you feel intuitively called to explore and write it here.

What are some of the stories I have about this quality?
(These can include recurring or powerful dreams, since the shadow shows up through the subconscious and symbols.)

What was my earliest experience with this quality?

What are some of the beliefs I formed as a result?

5 of Your Shadow Qualities

Refer to each of the qualities you explored in depth in the last few prompts.

The five shadow qualities I chose are:

1. Trigger:

2. Enamor:

3. Avoid:

4. Criticize:

5. Hold Back:

Exercise

Integrating Your Chosen Shadow Quality

From the last prompt on page 37, 5 of Your Shadow Qualities, you should have a list of qualities for each letter of TEACH. Now choose the quality you most want to integrate—the one that's currently impacting you the most. This can be a quality you dislike (like cowardice) or one that's generally praised and valued but that you don't feel comfortable owning (like charisma). The quality could also be associated with a challenge you're facing, or maybe it's just something you're curious about. Let your intuition point you in the right direction. For example, if you've chosen vulnerability, maybe your action is to have a tender conversation with a loved one about feelings that are difficult to share, such as the desire for more closeness, etc.

My shadow quality:

How is this quality a gift and asset to me?

What is one action I will take in the next three days to express this quality?

How do I envision my life would change if I integrated my shadow qualities?

MEDITATION

Coming to Know Your Shadow Quality

Use the QR code below to access a short meditation that will help you connect with your chosen shadow quality. You'll be guided to explore the stories and beliefs you've associated with this quality so that you can gain an awareness of how they impact your life.

STAGE 2:

SURRENDER

Alchemical Stage—DISSOLUTION:

When a substance in gaseous, liquid, or solid phase dissolves in a solvent to form a mixture known as a solution.

In shadow work, it can be viewed as the moment you choose to free yourself from an inauthentic identity that keeps you from wholeness and bogs you down in judgments you might have gained from family, society, etc.

✦ ✦ ✦

While the Awareness stage shines a light into the underground cave of your shadow to help you acknowledge what's there, **Surrender** is all about lowering yourself into this strange new realm and allowing for the element of surprise. Let down your defenses and allow for things to not be what they seem. A shadow quality that might have once elicited fear or alarm has the potential to become a friend or ally when you investigate further.

This is also the stage of shadow work where you start to release repressed emotions, many of which are the direct result of difficult events that got pushed down into your psyche. Surrender is like gazing directly into the flashing pairs of eyes in the dark cave. It can be scary as hell, but it's also deeply cathartic—sometimes even exhilarating. You will find yourself letting go of burdens you didn't even know you were carrying. Begin to move along with the as-yet-unexplored creatures inside your cave; set aside your judgments so you can see more clearly.

Understanding Surrender

Why is Surrender so difficult? The human brain is wired to want certainty and safety, even if the things we grasp at in order to feel secure are often the things that keep us from evolving into the highest version of who we are. If you're preoccupied with safety, which usually entails predictability and maintaining the status quo, you're probably not thinking about growth, which requires stretching into what's uncomfortable and unfamiliar.

This step of shadow work is crucial to growth because it means giving up what you've always known—and, in some cases, pieces of your self-created identity—in order to seek a deeper understanding of who you actually are.

A lot of people struggle with this step because they think Surrender is equivalent to throwing in the towel, quitting, and giving up your power. This isn't true!

Your power doesn't exist inside stubborn resistance, but in determined wholeness. In order to be whole, you have to actually *want* to expand your perception of who you are. You can only do that when you surrender a persona or role that's kept you trapped inside a box, because a box, even a safe, comfortable box with windows and a nice view, is still a box.

Coming to Acceptance

Surrender is a three-part process that is sandwiched between two other states—Resistance and Acceptance.

Resistance usually comes from a fear that's connected to a part of your self-created identity feeling like it's being directly threatened. The first stage of shadow work, Awareness, can help you get in touch with your resistance and its roots, but you also have to honor that instinct to resist—because you very likely have a good reason for it. For example, you may be afraid that you'll find something scary when you dig deep. You don't want to run the risk of finding an inner abuser or perpetrator, especially if you've felt hurt by an outer abuser or perpetrator. Be gentle with yourself here.

Surrender is releasing the idea that any of the shadow qualities are inherently good or bad. Sure, the actions someone might take when they connect with the part of them that is aggressive might end up being abusive, but that's a choice they made. The quality itself is neutral, and we're the ones who put the negative or positive charge on it. Surrender invites you to exercise curiosity about the quality, which leads to clarity.

If Surrender is about looking at the quality not through rose-colored glasses or dark shades but a clear view, **Acceptance** is about understanding and coming to terms with shadow qualities, like being lazy or a cheater. This doesn't mean you're lazy or that you cheat all the time. When you let go of the charge you have on the quality, you start to see how it presents in you. You see it's neither the demon nor the angel (since, obviously, positive qualities also live in your shadow) that you expected. Maybe it's just a little malnourished because it's been down in the dark for so long! With Acceptance comes the possibility of compassion.

This process of moving from Resistance to Surrender to Acceptance opens the door for new possibilities. You start to think, *At first it was really dark down here! But now that my eyes have adjusted, I'm starting to see it all in a new way.*

You've probably noticed that your judgments of others and the world at large are connected to what you judge within yourself. When you're in a state of intense judgment, the fear of reclaiming a quality gets intensified—because you may look at someone with that quality and be afraid of feeling toward yourself what you feel toward them.

This is when defensive statements like "I could never be like them!" or "I'm nothing like them!" start to rear their ugly heads. But such defenses are self-defeating. It's like putting on armor to fight an invisible enemy—one who actually lives inside you and needs your compassion and respect.

Surrendering your judgments takes away the charge of fear or hatred. It helps you step into the space of your soul, where you get to reclaim what's yours and express it in your life consciously, in the ways that serve you best.

One of the most important aspects of Surrender is feeling safe enough to go to the places you fear. This often looks like giving yourself space and time to feel your feelings, knowing it's only natural that fear will come up—and even though your Resistance may cause you to go into fight-or-flight, you're safe.

You can remind yourself of this as you dive into the prompts, exercise, and meditation. For example, you can take a few minutes to engage in a simple practice like standing on the earth with your bare feet to ground yourself, listening to soothing music, taking a bath or shower in candlelight, visualizing a place or person you love, etc. Whatever safety feels like for you, give yourself permission to move toward it.

JOURNAL PROMPTS

Surrender

Surrendering to Surrender

How I feel about surrender:

In the past, when I've surrendered, I experienced:

Surrender can feel scary because:

Surrender can feel exhilarating because:

From Resistance
to Acceptance, Part 1

Reflect on the shadow quality you chose in the Awareness stage, from page 38, Exercise: Integrating Your Chosen Shadow Quality. Keep in mind that this quality may
be "positive" or "negative," but it will definitely still be
attached to fears and judgments. Be compassionate as you
dig into those.

The shadow quality I'm choosing to integrate is:

How do I resist this quality?

What are my judgments of this quality?

How is this quality a reflection of the ways I am judging myself and others?

What is it about this quality I fear?

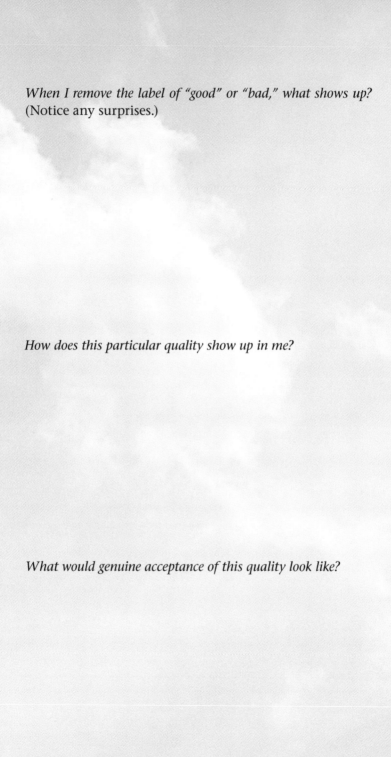

When I remove the label of "good" or "bad," what shows up?
(Notice any surprises.)

How does this particular quality show up in me?

What would genuine acceptance of this quality look like?

What would it take for me to accept this quality as part of my inner landscape?

How can I give myself permission to get in touch with and befriend this quality in ways that serve me?

From Resistance
to Acceptance, Part 2

If you chose a negative shadow quality in Part 1, such as cowardice or self-delusion (something you're triggered by, or that you criticize, or perhaps that you avoid), choose a positive shadow quality, which you identified on page 37, Journal Prompt: 5 of Your Shadow Qualities, this time around. This will be something you are enamored by, like confidence, or perhaps something you hold back from, like enthusiasm. If you chose a positive shadow quality in Part 1, now choose a negative shadow quality.

The second shadow quality I'm exploring is:

How do I resist this quality?

What are my judgments of this quality?

How is this quality a reflection of the ways I am judging myself and others?

What is it about this quality I fear?

When I remove the label of "good" or "bad," what shows up?
(Notice any surprises.)

How does this particular quality show up in me?

What would genuine acceptance of this quality look like?

What would it take for me to accept this quality as part of my inner landscape?

How can I give myself permission to get in touch with and befriend this quality in ways that serve me?

EXERCISE

Embodying Acceptance

Refer back to the two qualities that you explored over the last few pages.

Are the two qualities I chose connected in any way? For example, maybe you chose confidence as the quality you're enamored with and shyness as the one you're triggered by. These clearly present as opposites. *What does that tell you about what you value and what you've relegated to your shadow?*

What can I do to honor and accept both qualities?

What is one action I will take in the next three days to express these qualities?

MEDITATION

Sweet Surrender

Use the QR code below to access a short meditation that will help you feel into your specific resistance and surrender to being with your chosen shadow quality in a value-neutral way so you can reclaim it as part of you. Do this meditation twice (once for the positive quality and once for the negative one you've elected to work with).

STAGE 3:
RESPONSIBILITY

Alchemical Stage—SEPARATION:

The conversion of a mixture of chemical substances into separate blends for the purpose of extracting a "pure" essence.

In shadow work, this is the stage where we separate from old, unhelpful patterns and defensive responses to the shadow. We look at our own response-ability and use it to purify our relationship with our wholeness.

✦ ✦ ✦

By the time you get to **Responsibility**, you see that you can liberate yourself from your triggers and connect with what lives below the hotbed of reactive emotions inside of you. This is where you really start to activate the gifts of your shadow. You can't do that until you forgive yourself for anything that's still serving to keep your shadow qualities shoved way down, where you can't access them.

It all begins with self-forgiveness, and it culminates in making a conscious choice to move forward without the baggage of the past weighing on you. With forgiveness, you can learn from your shadow and take responsibility for how you express your shadow qualities in the world, thus liberating yourself from difficult emotions that may have kept you trapped.

When the Shadow Takes Over

We all have moments when the shadow takes us over, and our logical, rational self no longer seems to be the one in charge. You may have experienced this yourself: maybe in a spontaneous temper tantrum where you lashed out at a loved one or an addiction that became a spell you couldn't break out of, or a single fateful moment in which you managed to blow up your life. These are the times you're left in a mental tailspin, scratching your head wondering how the hell you ended up here. You'll say, "What just happened? That wasn't me!"

But it *was* you. Or at least it was a part of you that had become so invisible, it had no choice but to leap up and say, "Hellloooo! I'm here!"

These moments might feel scary, but remember, the shadow is a beautiful messenger that expresses emotional truth over appearances of perfection. The only reason it acts out is that it's yearning for you to move toward a truer version of you.

Think about the times when you say things like, "I should . . . ," "I shouldn't . . . ," "I will always . . . ," "I will never . . ." These rigid, absolute statements have more to do with your fears and judgments than the reality of who you are, what you feel, and what you want. The shadow can often be found in such pronouncements—which is why most of us end up acting like hypocrites, even when we have the best intentions. We set lofty standards that have so little to do with the lives we truly want to live— creating goals and honoring values that might not even be based on our inner compass and desires.

If you can think of a time when your shadow acted out and you did something out of character, join the club—because you're not alone.

It's not easy to face up to doing or saying things you've been conditioned to view as unforgivable or outside the status quo, and that might have had a negative impact on you and others. At the same time, when does someone do something unforgivable? Usually, it's not because they're innately bad, but because they've shoved parts of their identity into the darkness. How would you like it if someone told you to hide out in a dark closet where you never get a chance to come out and see the light of day? Well, that's how your shadow qualities feel!

Remember Debbie Ford's beach-ball effect from the Introduction: the more you suppress something, the more likely it is to bounce back and hit you. Only when you are aware of your emotions and triggers can you find balance, like a beach ball floating on a wave.

In fact, even if you've acted "unforgivably" in the past, it's a good idea to thank and acknowledge your shadow—because although it may not have done it in the most skillful way, it's always there to help you recognize when you're not in alignment. It's there to give you a kick in the butt and remind you to get connected to your innermost truth.

The Initiation

The Responsibility stage of shadow work is an important initiation. When you go through an initiation, you cease to be the same person you used to be. You walk through a portal that takes you into a more mature version of you—one that's no longer a victim of circumstance.

When you take responsibility, you strengthen your core self instead of being pulled every which way by your reactions to the outside world. When you get triggered, you see it as an opportunity to become curious about why. And it stops being about seeing yourself through someone else's eyes; it's about how *you* feel, not how you're perceived by *others*.

Instead of being so *other*-referenced—"He yelled at me. . . . She made me feel small. . . . They did something I didn't like. . . ."—you become *self*-referenced —"Wow, I feel crappy. . . . What are the stories I'm telling myself that are causing me to feel this way? How do I want to respond to this situation? How can I do it in a way that empowers me?"

You might still be triggered and see plenty of things in other people that could use some improvement, but now, instead of being so activated by what's outside of you, it becomes easier to keep your attention on yourself and what you're doing to make sense of the situation.

How do you do this? Through forgiveness for what you've done or not done, said or not said. Not only do you forgive yourself for your unskillful actions, but you also apologize to the parts of yourself that you blamed for getting you into trouble. You say "I'm sorry" to the parts that you shoved into the darkness. Sorry for not recognizing them as sacred teachers and ignoring their wisdom because it scared you. Sorry for closing yourself off, which caused you to harm both yourself and others in ways that you're still uncovering.

Ultimately, you're not forgiving yourself for doing something *wrong*, but because you didn't listen to your shadow qualities or recognize their gifts, which is the very thing that led to pain and disappointment. It's only when you forgive yourself that you start to free the gift of your shadow qualities. You realize crisis is a catalyst for growth.

Some people resist forgiveness because they think it means condoning the crappy things that are best left in the past. But forgiveness is what frees you. When you're not spending energy beating yourself up, you start to use that energy to act in ways that honor your values. You don't get sidelined by a shadow quality that's lurking underground, silently raging for not being included in your life—because you're much more open to the wisdom it has to share with you.

When you offer yourself forgiveness, you are transformed. You've finally stepped through the portal, and you're not the same person anymore. You start to be in active, loving conversation with those figures that were lingering in the cave of your shadow. All of this makes you *want* to be responsible.

In the Responsibility stage, it becomes easier to pay attention to the voices inside you before they become a deafening roar. Instead of shutting them down or shoving them deeper, you start to ask them what they need and want. Imagine yourself literally talking to them: "Oh, you need some down time, but I've been working long hours. I totally get this might cause problems down the line, so before we crash and burn, I'm going to take time for rest and relaxation."

Also, responsibility means getting brutally honest with where you might be taking too much of it! By now, you are so steeped in self-compassion that you begin to address the things you've been doing out of guilt or obligation that are not ultimately serving you or others.

JOURNAL PROMPTS

Responsibility

Receiving Forgiveness

A difficult time in my childhood when I did something my care-givers considered wrong taught me this about forgiveness:

I learned that I could only be forgiven if:

I have difficulty forgiving myself when:

I find it easy to forgive myself when:

Where I Need to Forgive Myself

What do I still need to forgive myself for?

Here are all the reasons I haven't forgiven myself for that situation:

What is the shadow quality I associate with this situation?
(For example, it might be something like ignorance or
misplaced trust.)

How does not forgiving myself hold me back and keep me from
growing and taking responsibility for this shadow quality in a
deeper way?

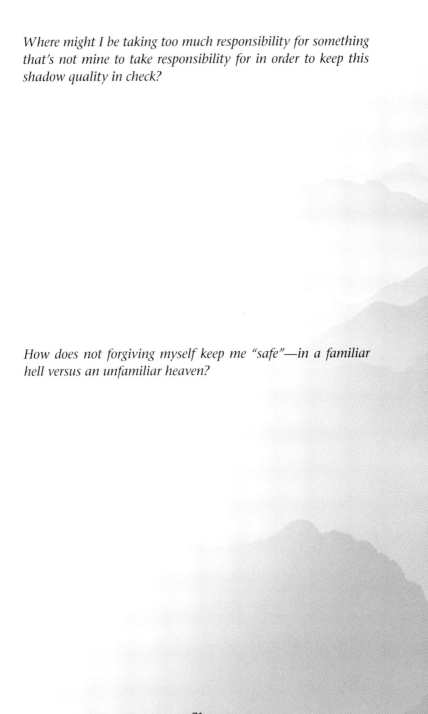

Where might I be taking too much responsibility for something that's not mine to take responsibility for in order to keep this shadow quality in check?

How does not forgiving myself keep me "safe"—in a familiar hell versus an unfamiliar heaven?

How might it feel to forgive myself? (Don't worry if you're not there yet, just imagine what it might feel like.)

Here are all the reasons to forgive myself:

*Here's how that experience I find it hard to forgive myself for
helped me:*

Here's what I learned about what to do differently:

EXERCISE

I Am That

Standing in your responsibility starts with acknowledging that you're a powerful co-creator of your reality. Look into a mirror for two to three minutes and repeat to yourself, "I am [fill in the blank with your shadow quality that you haven't forgiven yourself for]." This might sound like, "I am ignorant" or "I am gullible."

Remember, although you may attach judgments to this quality, the quality is neither good nor bad. Please be compassionate yet unrelenting as you claim whatever the quality is. Notice the feelings and stay with them—they will gradually start to neutralize and subside. When you feel more neutral, notice whether there's anything about your judgment that has changed. Now respond to the following prompts:

The gift of my chosen shadow quality is:

In recognizing the gift of this shadow quality, here's how I'm reclaiming it and committing to doing things differently. (For examples, "When I'm tempted to lie to others, I'll notice this means I'm trying to protect myself. In the future I will remember it's okay to be discerning about what I express.")

What are some alternative ways to stand in my truth?

MEDITATION

Self-Forgiveness

Use the QR code below to access a short meditation that will help you connect with the healing, transformative balm of forgiveness. You'll make contact with a disowned part of yourself that needs your attention and forgiveness, and then you'll make a conscious choice as to how you'll engage it in future—in a way that aligns with your deepest values and moves you toward empowerment and self-connection.

STAGE 4:
AUTHENTICITY

Alchemical Stage—CONJUNCTION:

The process of combining the elements from the previous three stages and making a decision about what's valuable and what you intend to keep.

In shadow work, the elements you choose to keep are the ones that hearken back to the truth of who you are. The conscious and unconscious components form a single essence that represents the union of dualities: your true self.

✦ ✦ ✦

Authenticity is the practice of bringing the treasures back up from the shadowy depths of the cave and allowing them to soak up the sunlight of your conscious life. This is when you start to actively embody your quest to know and honor your shadow qualities instead of stashing pieces of yourself underground.

Authenticity can feel extremely vulnerable, but it's also deeply empowering. You might end up feeling like a shaky newborn as you coordinate the "opposites" in your personality—encompassing both the negative traits you dislike or fear as well the positive ones you might feel too intimidated to claim for yourself—and find a point of balance. Exercising radical honesty can sometimes look like face-planting in the middle of self-expression as you navigate what can feel like extremes in your personality, but you'll start to become more confident as you go through the process.

Authenticity isn't something you can fake. In truth, the hard part is removing the obstacles that keep you from expressing it. Once you've gone through the first few layers of shadow work and removed any giant boulders standing in the way, you'll no longer feel like there's something to hide.

This step is an invitation for you to accept the both/and instead of the either/or of your life. This makes it necessary to move beyond preconceived ideas about authenticity. Maybe you've always seen yourself as cool and witty with a dry sense of humor—but the person looking back at you in the mirror is a sloppy, stammering bundle of tears and tender emotions. It can be unsettling to accept this less-polished version of yourself—it doesn't project the image you'd like others to see, but it is authentic.

You'll soon discover that authenticity is about all the parts of that you are working in a unified way, such that nothing needs to take the back seat. All voices in the chorus of you get a chance to be heard.

Self-Trust: The Key to Authenticity

You've definitely felt it before: the burst of spontaneity and joy that emerges when you're just being you. Maybe the things you've done or said in this joyful state have even surprised you! It takes an enormous amount of self-trust to be here, but it's paradoxically effortless when you're not constantly censoring yourself.

Self-trust isn't about mulling over every single thing you say or decision you're going to make, like there's a right or wrong you need to dig deep for. It's a permission you give yourself. Self-trust is a solid commitment not to hide any parts of yourself in order to be loved or accepted.

And self-trust isn't just an internal belief that anchors you in authenticity; it's constantly activated through the process of truth-telling.

This is where things can get tricky. In the era of social media, we have a lot of people telling us to trust ourselves, to be vulnerable, to get real. However, in many cases, authenticity has become a performance—something that's contrived, manufactured, and manipulated in order to get more likes and follows. Social media has taught us there's a formula for authenticity. But if you're trying to play by those rules, it means you're still other-referenced, not self-referenced.

Instead of checking in with what feels true for you, you might be basing your authenticity on how you've seen others expressing themselves. "On the one hand, I want to be honest—but I don't want to show up without makeup and start crying all of a sudden. OMG, does that mean I'm out of touch with my emotions?"

Don't compare your insides to someone else's out-sides. There's a whole system of algorithms and incentives that have created our current, filtered understanding of authenticity, and in most cases, it's premeditated.

This is also where it's important for you to remember the value of staying really close to how you're feeling.

Ever heard the term vulnerability hangover? According to Dr. Brené Brown, it's "the gut-wrenching feeling of shame and fear that pops right after we undertake an emotional risk." Of course, putting yourself out there can be deeply rewarding, but context matters. You don't have to go from zero to 60 by rushing into a TMI conversation. Authenticity isn't about laying every single one of your cards on the table and forcibly unmasking yourself. Exercise discernment as well as care and appreciation for your tender parts. Privacy might be an aspect of your authenticity, depending on what's going on in your life—so don't feel the need to get naked for everything and everyone!

Authenticity Is the Basis for Connection

It can be tough to build a foundation of self-trust if you're antsy about telling the truth. But if you don't share what's true for you, you begin to build resentment toward yourself (for hiding) and others (for being content with the teeniest sliver of who you are).

We're conditioned with this warped idea that going along with something we don't feel 100 percent on board with is the best path forward—often because it means we'll avoid confrontation or disagreement or we'll gain acceptance or love.

Let's say your partner loves Marvel movies, and you're not into them. Agreeing to watch the latest Avengers flick just to please them isn't going to get you very far in the connection department. We tend to believe that sharing the truth about how we feel will alienate us from other people, but when you withhold the truth, you withhold the very thing that will enhance your connection with another.

So, the next time you're invited to spend a couple hours watching superheroes save the world, tell the truth. You might say, "I don't like Marvel movies, but I'm happy to sit next to you as I watch something on my iPad" or "I've never been into the superhero thing, but I'll watch this movie with you because I love seeing how much you love it."

What's powerful about authenticity is that the options are endless when you start telling the truth. First, though, it requires staying true to yourself, not being a chameleon to please others. Authenticity also has the capacity to bring you into greater intimacy with *yourself,* especially as you start integrating your shadow qualities.

The integration part requires care and calibration. The funny thing about us humans is that we tend to swing to extremes when we try on a new way of being. For example, let's say confidence is one of your chosen shadow qualities. You might worry that if you start bringing confidence into your self-expression, you'll start acting cocky or arrogant (of course, the next step here is to go back down into your cave and reclaim cockiness and arrogance). You might be concerned about the inevitable self-judgment and judgment from others.

This is an amazing opportunity to reconcile with all parts of who you are so that you no longer consent to abandon yourself. What's possible when this happens? You become more conscious of *who* you're giving the microphone to at any given time. You treasure the cocky confidence as well as the shy sensitivity—and you start to value what happens when either of them talk.

A lot of times, you probably stop short of expressing various parts of yourself. Maybe there's a fear that if you do, the people you care about will feel hurt or even leave. But you have an opportunity to investigate the next layer. That is, what would happen if you expressed yourself and they left? Could it mean that the relationship wasn't what you thought it was and you're opening up space for something that's truer and better aligned?

JOURNAL PROMPTS

Authenticity

Honoring My Authentic No

What places in my life am I finding myself saying yes when I want to say no?

What are the benefits of saying yes when I want to say no?

What are the drawbacks of saying yes when I want to say no?

Honoring My Authentic Yes

What places in my life am I saying no when I want to say yes?

What are the benefits of saying no when I want to say yes?

What are the drawbacks of saying no when I want to say yes?

STORIES FROM MY HEAD AND MY HEART
Saying Yes When I Want to Say No

Choose a situation where you might be feeling stuck saying yes where you want to say no and write out the story you're telling yourself about the situation in your mind.
(For example: "The story my head tells me is that I have to put up with my partner's bad behavior—because if I don't, I'll be all alone, which is way worse.")

The story my head tells me is:

Take a moment to connect with your body by placing a hand on your chest to draw out the deeper truth and write out the truth of the situation from your heart.
(For example: "The truth my heart tells me is that I'm dishonoring myself by staying in a relationship where I don't feel met or heard—and that if I continue to do so, I'll lose myself.")

The truth my heart tells me is:

STORIES FROM MY HEAD AND MY HEART
Saying Yes When I Want to Say No

Choose a situation where you might be feeling stuck saying no where you want to say yes and write out the story you're telling yourself about the situation in your mind.

The story my head tells me is:

Take a moment to connect with your body by placing a hand on your chest to draw out the deeper truth and write out the truth of the situation from your heart.

The truth my heart tells me is:

STORIES FROM MY HEAD AND MY HEART
Holding Back My Truth

Choose a situation where you might be holding back from sharing who you truly are, and how you truly feel, from the people in your life.

The story my head tells me is:

Take a moment to connect with your body by placing a hand on your chest to draw out the deeper truth and write out the truth of the situation from your heart.

The truth my heart tells me is:

STORIES FROM MY HEAD AND MY HEART
Fear of Taking Action

Choose a situation where you might feel frightened of taking action in your life that could lead to growth but that's filled with uncertainty.

The story my head tells me is:
Take a moment to connect with your body by placing a

hand on your chest to draw out the deeper truth and write out the truth of the situation from your heart.

The truth my heart tells me is:

STORIES FROM MY HEAD AND MY HEART
Fear of What Your Want

Choose a situation where you want something that you and others might have judged as unrealistic, impractical, wrong, or foolish.

The story my head tells me is:

Take a moment to connect with your body by placing a hand on your chest to draw out the deeper truth and write out the truth of the situation from your heart.

The truth my heart tells me is:

STORIES FROM MY HEAD AND MY HEART
Fear of Inner Conflict

Choose a situation where you feel a sense of inner conflict that you just can't seem to resolve.

The story my head tells me is:

Take a moment to connect with your body by placing a hand on your chest to draw out the deeper truth and write out the truth of the situation from your heart.

The truth my heart tells me is:

Exercise

Your Shadow Ally

Choose one of the truths your heart told you from the prompts in the last section, Stories from My Head and My Heart. Briefly skim through them and go with the one that makes your heart pound a little harder and faster than the others. Now pick any one of the shadow qualities you identified in the earlier sections of this journal. By now, you'll have two or three: one that triggers you, one that you're enamored by but find it hard to express, and possibly a unique third quality you worked to forgive yourself for in the Responsibility stage. You should be able to find these on page 38, Exercise: Integrating Your Chosen Shadow Quality; page 52, Journal Prompt: From Resistance to Acceptance, Part 2; and page 68, Journal Prompt: Where I Need to Forgive Myself.

You'll choose one of these qualities as an ally to help you express the truth you identified. Check in with your body as you go through each of these qualities. You'll immediately feel which is the right one to work with—perhaps as a flutter in your gut, an opening in your heart, or some other sensation. Your body is the barometer of your truth, and you'll feel it within, even before a thought kicks up. Get used to paying attention to your body, because it's where your truth lives!

My shadow quality I'm choosing to be my ally in truth:

Next, get quiet, settle in, and listen to what the shadow quality is communicating. If this situation feels in any way difficult, remind yourself, "It's safe for me to talk to my shadow qualities. My shadow qualities have a lot of wisdom for me, and I'm willing to communicate with them so I can find the light in this situation." This will probably come through sensations in your body. Allow yourself to write down your responses without thinking too hard about them. Give yourself time to let it flow.

What specific ways can this shadow quality help me express my truth to myself and others?

How can I call upon this shadow quality consciously for support or guidance?

Set a date for expressing your truth to someone safe, with the help of the shadow quality you've chosen.

I will share my truth on _____ with _____
                        [date]   [person or people].

MEDITATION

Tending to Your Authentic Self

Use the QR code below to access a short meditation that will help you reconnect with any of the parts of yourself that you may have inadvertently abandoned. This process will also entail coming back to your body, the barometer of your truth, to ask questions like: *What do I think? What do I feel? What do I want? What do I need?* By consciously calling in your abandoned parts, you'll discover that you have greater access to your intuition and your truth.

STAGE 5:
RESILIENCE

ALCHEMICAL STAGE—FERMENTATION:

The process during which sugar molecules are broken into simpler compounds to make substances that contribute to generating chemical energy.

In shadow work, this is the falling-away of the old self and the emergence of the true self. While the first four stages were about transmuting your inauthentic, fragmented self, this stage is about letting the last remnants of who you used to be fall away.

✦ ✦ ✦

We come to **Resilience**—which is inner strength in the face of life's inevitable curveballs. Shadow work is about realizing that you're a phoenix, with the power to rise from the ashes of your former self.

This is where you'll be testing your authenticity in the real world, with the recognition that you may still encounter some cringe moments that could kick up the dust of shame and fear, not to mention the desire to banish your shadow qualities back to the cave of your psyche. However, resilience will help you move in the direction of wholeness no matter what.

Shadow Commitments

Resilience is about your commitment to follow through with what you started in the authenticity stage: to express your truth, even in the face of old fears and shadow beliefs. But it's likely that throughout this process, you may still experience self-doubt and stuckness.

This is where *shadow commitments*, or underlying commitments, come into play. When there's a discrepancy between what you say you want—in this case, authentic expression—and the way your life is actually going, that usually means there's a shadow commitment just beneath the surface.

How do shadow commitments cause problems? It's impossible to commit to being your whole self if you've already committed to something else. It's like making vows at the altar when your heart is secretly burning for someone else—a fact you may not even consciously realize.

What you think or say you're committed to can sometimes be at odds with that deeper commitment you're holding in your unconscious mind. You believe you want one thing, but you're secretly committed to its opposite.

As you will see, there's usually a very good reason a shadow commitment is in place.

We all have shadow commitments that originated as promises we made to ourselves in childhood, usually as the result of a limiting shadow belief. We made those promises to stay safe or feel loved.

Consciously, you want to travel toward the beautiful vision of authenticity you've unearthed, but you unconsciously set your internal GPS to a different course. No matter what plans you make, you continue to double back onto the route that feels safe and familiar instead of forging ahead on the path that aligns with your goals.

For example, you want to quit your job and start a business that's aligned with your authentic self—the one who's committed to letting each part shine. However, you can't get traction because your shadow commitment is to stay safe and small. You manage to make some moves, but there's another part of you that sabotages those efforts and causes you to end up saying things like "Maybe I'm not cut out for this." You're disappointed, and at the same time, the part of you that formed the shadow commitment gets to stay safe and refrain from taking any risks to help you achieve your dream.

Some common behaviors that could indicate the presence of a shadow commitment are:

- Staying silent
- Staying small
- Remaining invisible
- Not speaking your mind (even when it's connected to something you feel passionate about)
- Accepting struggle as a way of life
- Believing you have to "do it all on my own"
- Seeking comfort over growth

If you see these behaviors in yourself, dig deep into the "why" behind your choices to expose the shadow commitment underneath. At some point, you'll have to decide it's time to move on from the shadow commitment and redirect your energy toward what you want. The most powerful choices you can make are the ones that realign you with your authentic desires and with the essence of your whole self, which is bigger than fear or self-sabotage.

The Power of Alignment

Many people think resilience is connected to a warrior mentality: we put it on like armor, then we connect to a strict regimen powered by discipline and sheer will.

Willpower might serve you in many respects, but it has its limitations. Authenticity isn't about willpower because authenticity isn't something you have to force. Authenticity is merely the act of aligning with your wholeness.

Aligning with your wholeness doesn't mean life is going to become a castle in the sky where everything goes according to plan. It just means you become more comfortable dissolving your shadow commitments, which can be decidedly *un*comfortable, at least at first. This can look like breaking off certain relationships, changing jobs, moving locations, etc. However, you start to navigate change with more confidence and ease because you see that when you commit to your wholeness, the world around you ultimately catches up with that internal alignment.

Getting aligned with yourself requires identifying those shadow commitments, and no amount of muscling through will get you there. Once you know how to do it, you won't need willpower because it starts to become effortless.

Let's say you want more heart-centered relationships. But when you get quiet and check in with yourself, you realize you're not pursuing those relationships because you're more committed to never experiencing rejection! You think to yourself, *This sucks. Rejection is painful—and I really don't want to have to face it! But . . . I definitely know I want heart-centered relationships. Is it worth the struggle, though?*

In this scenario, you've done a lot of work to keep yourself safe and small. You're content not to express your true needs in return for relationships in which you don't feel met and supported—all so you won't be rejected. Without you realizing it, *you are rejecting yourself* instead. By abandoning what you really want in order to stay connected to people who are totally oblivious, you have rejected your own desires for authentic, heart-centered connection, letting the shadow commitment rule your actions.

A lot of times, what we most fear tends to be external —for example, the fear of being rejected, abandoned, canceled, hated—and we attempt to avoid it at all costs. We neglect to see that what we fear is *already* happening on the inside, which is even more damaging.

Once you are aware not just of your shadow commitment, but also of the ways you've been unwittingly hurting yourself, getting into alignment with your true self will become a lot easier. Willpower won't work here. Believing you can follow Nike's advice and "just do it" often ends up leading down a spiral of shame and despair.

If you feel shame over a lack of alignment with your authenticity, take heart—because there's an incredible opportunity here.

At the root of shame is a belief that often sounds like "If you knew this about me, you wouldn't love me." Flip this to "*I* know this about me, and *I* still love me." If you can get to that place, whatever judgments may come from the outside will have no effect on you whatsoever.

When you keep doing the forgiveness work you started in the responsibility stage, you defuse the power that shame once had over you. Instead of getting stuck on the willpower treadmill, you muster the courage to face yourself. That's when you see that your shadow commitment isn't serving you, and you align with a new commitment that will.

When Debbie Ford was on *The Oprah Winfrey Show* for the first time, she became anxious before going onstage. She came up with a mantra that helped her stay calm and centered throughout her appearance: "Even if I suck, I will love myself anyway."

And that's what resilience is: the commitment to loving yourself anyway, no matter what happens, because you're no longer willing to jump ship and abandon your true self.

JOURNAL PROMPTS

Resilience

My Shadow Commitments

How am I holding back from my authentic thoughts, feelings, and values? (You can usually identify this by looking at the places in your life where you feel stuck.)

What are some of the things keeping me from expressing authenticity?

What are some of the stories I'm continuing to tell myself about the challenges of authenticity?

What are the shadow commitments I've made to myself that hold me back?

How did these shadow commitments keep me safe at one point in my life? (Remember, shadow commitments aren't bad— in most cases, you made them with the best of intentions, often for the sake of survival.)

How are these shadow commitments causing me to abandon myself and my wholeness today?

Aligning with Possibility

Now choose one shadow commitment you identified in the last set of prompts and write it below.

What would be possible if I align with what I truly desire instead of letting my shadow commitment hold me back? (Make a list of as many things as you can think of. Whatever you come up with should be connected to your most authentic expression of self—like leaving a toxic job or relationship, moving to a new place, following a dream you abandoned a few years ago, etc.—but that you've found challenging to bring into your life.)

What is the new commitment I'm making to align with my authenticity?

Exercise

Your Resilience Affirmation

Write down a simple one-sentence affirmation you can repeat to yourself throughout the day as a reminder of the new commitment you're making (for example, "I'm committed to visibility instead of hiding"). This will be the affirmation that strengthens your resilience. You might wish to put it on your phone, computer, or anywhere else you'll see it frequently. Say it out loud at least once a day and let the words vibrate throughout your being.

My Resilience Affirmation:

The action I'll take to bring my resilience affirmation to life is:

MEDITATION

Dismantling Your Shadow Commitment

Use the QR code below to access a short meditation that will help you integrate your Resilience affirmation and new commitment into your conscious and unconscious mind. This process will also help you acknowledge and honor the shadow commitment that may have been keeping you in its protective grip. But from now on, you're no longer content to stay safe and small—you're allowing yourself to make full body and soul contact with the world as you commit to aligning with your authenticity.

STAGE 6:
NOURISHMENT

ALCHEMICAL STAGE—DISTILLATION:

The boiling and condensing, heating and cooling, of a substance to purify it.

In shadow work, you extract the essential meaning of your journey to actualize your spirit and assimilate your shadow qualities.

✦ ✦ ✦

You've come to the **Nourishment** stage of your journey. Shadow work is a continuous process of distilling what you've learned—purifying your spirit as the ancient alchemists purified base metals by turning them into gold. This particular stage is a delicate yet intentional act of readjusting, adapting, and continuing to dip back into the cave to discover more of yourself. As you harmonize your inner and outer worlds, your consciousness expands. You step into and welcome even more of yourself on this journey home to your essence.

It's similar to propping open a door so you have access to your conscious and unconscious self—and in your commitment to being more of who you really are, you let yourself be nourished by this space of permission and genuine intimacy with all parts of you.

Desire Isn't a Dirty Word

In order to experience the gifts of nourishment, you have to be willing to acknowledge that you have needs. However, knowing your needs isn't enough. A lot of us are taught to get our needs met at the lowest possible threshold, which can look like meeting our survival needs only. Food, shelter, basic safety—check.

However, to truly nourish yourself, it's essential to go beyond that threshold of *need* and into *want*. This is desire, the place where your soul's passion for purpose, meaning, and fulfillment feels the strongest and most alive. When you live inside desire, not from lack or desperation but from the recognition that the presence of desire is its own fulfillment, you stop depriving yourself. You realize that desire keeps you attuned to your soul's authentic yearnings. And you discover just how many of those yearnings have been tossed into the cave of your shadow.

That kind of yearning is a *shadow desire*—a strong desire you've been resisting for a long time. We tend to resist it because it's the purest kind of wanting—the kind that may have nothing to do with being good or lovable or acceptable or any of the things we're conditioned to seek in order to feel safe and like we belong. In order to know your wholeness, you must be willing to reclaim not just ordinary desires, but also shadow desires.

Sadly, many of us are not taught to trust our desire. Maybe you were told that following desire is sinful, selfish, or unwise. Maybe you've convinced yourself that it's greedy to ask for what you want, let alone have what you want. Or you think putting someone else's needs or desires ahead of your own makes you a good person.

Many of us also tend to get caught up in the fear that we can't have what we want, so why bother? It's possible that at some point, you convinced yourself it would be too painful to want something you'll never end up getting. This is why, so often, when you tap into a genuine desire, you may end up dismissing it and giving yourself a long list of reasons for why you aren't worthy of it or why others deserve it more than you do. These are tricks your mind plays to keep you from feeling the magnitude of your desire.

Desire is not bad, irresponsible, or selfish. In fact, it's one of the greatest tools to support you in your shadow work. It'll help you fill your own cup and ditch your people-pleasing ways so you can feel a sense of sturdiness from within.

Shadow work is about engaging the panorama of your whole self and honoring the abundance that lives within you. The abundance of your inner world always mirrors the abundance of your outer world. Your desire is here to remind you that if you feel it, a way to meet it already exists!

The universe is an abundant place that's more than capable of giving you what you want and need. But first, you have to be more comfortable feeling and acknowledging desires—and recognizing that you're worthy of having them fulfilled.

If you're sitting there thinking, *I have no idea what I desire!*, that's another sign the information you seek is hidden in the cave, waiting for you to dive down and retrieve it. In truth, every single person innately knows what they desire, but for all the aforementioned reasons, most of us have repressed that knowing over time—usually, because we feel we must restrain or restrict ourselves from going overboard.

Think about your own tendencies. Do you deprive yourself of what you need—which might include asking for help or taking some necessary time off to relax—because you fear tipping over into self-indulgence or dependency? If you slam on the brakes of your desire, you risk starving yourself, both figuratively and literally. And when you starve yourself, you run the risk of becoming resentful or afraid of your desire. Maybe you convince yourself it's not important, but that doesn't mean it isn't there, lurking in the shadows, gathering the energy to rise up so you'll finally pay attention.

Eating at the Banquet of Nourishment

Beyond ignoring many of your desires outright, it's possible you've also grown accustomed to thinking your desires can only be fulfilled a certain way. Often we fall into the trap of assuming someone or something outside of us will be the source of the nourishment we seek.

Maybe you've had the experience of your desire being coaxed to the surface by a lover, a hobby, or a job you were passionate about, or something else—and then something changed, and that external motivation or excitement ran out, leaving you with an empty feeling. For many of us, the experience of coming alive with a passionate desire changes us forever . . . but if the cause of our aliveness was external, losing it can be painful. In fact, it can send your desire into hiding for long stretches of time.

Your task is to cultivate a relationship with desire by meeting it. You're meant to feast at the banquet table of nourishment. And even if one source of nourishment runs out, that doesn't mean you can't experience fulfillment in other ways.

A lot of us are taught to value delayed gratification and deprive ourselves of pleasure—to save the gorgeous dress hanging in the closet for a special occasion instead of treating every moment of life as a special occasion! The message you unconsciously take in when you wait for something or someone to give you cause for celebration is "I'm not worthy of doing this for myself, for the sake of feeling pleasure."

There's nothing wrong with delayed gratification—building anticipation can be great—but if it's a way of life, it's likely you'll end up constantly moving the goalposts for what you want and when you'll get to *have* what you want. You'll set up elaborate rewards systems but constantly stay shy of truly achieving what you desire—or you'll use that rewards system as a way to beat yourself up instead of to enhance your enjoyment.

Nourishment is intrinsically tied to the primal relationship we have to mothering—which could mean the mother who raised you or just your own connection to "maternal" qualities of nurturance, safety, validation, etc. Many of us are propelled by a sense of lack that we inherited from our earliest memories of what nurturing looked like. When you were extremely young, you didn't see yourself as being separate from your mother—and even if you weren't conscious of it, your ideas about worth and nourishment emerged from how she met your physical and emotional needs as well as her own.

You step into your own source of nourishment when you're able to separate from the way someone else—including your mom—chose to nourish you. Instead, you move toward what *you* find most nourishing. Nourishment also entails enjoying the life cycle of a pleasurable moment or experience—instead of speeding through it or not being present for all parts of it, you savor it in its entirety.

It's important to clarify that nourishing yourself doesn't mean you're going to just do everything on your own. It means you're willing to be honest and authentic about what you desire, which means you stand a better chance of increasing intimacy and connection with others. Your desire is a core part of who you are, and it actually makes you more attractive to others when you're able to own it and invite the world to help you fulfill it. While the first step is to stand in your desire instead of abandoning it, you further nourish yourself by enlisting the help of others.

Making a desire-based request is a powerful act of self-nourishment because it means you're affirming what you want. You're saying, "I deserve to have this." A desire-based request is robust enough to take no for an answer and to collaborate for a win-win instead of shrinking in the face of rejection. In contrast, if you're still basing your source of nourishment on someone or something else, the way you ask might end up being tinged by hesitation or dismissiveness. Don't let the self-punishing voice trick you out of going for what you want—whether you're doing it for yourself or inviting another to be part of your experience.

JOURNAL PROMPTS

Nourishment

What I Feel Nourished By

How does nourishment feel in my body?

What are the sources of nourishment in my life?

How do I go about meeting my needs, especially those needs that are connected with pleasure and nourishment (For example: asking for help, doing it on my own, doing it when I'm not busy with work, not feeling deserving of meeting my needs, expecting others will do that work for me, etc.)?

How did my mother or maternal figure nourish me or not?

What did I learn from them about nourishment and needs?

My Relationship to Desire

What was a time in my childhood when I really wanted something—candy, a toy, a trip? How did I share this with my caregivers? What was their reaction?

How is that situation connected to my current associations with desire?

Over my life, what deep desires have I let myself fulfill?

Why do I choose to fulfill these desires?

My Shadow Desires

What are the shadow desires I have that I deprive myself of fulfilling or that I resist?

Why do I choose not to fulfill these desires?

What shadow desire has been around for a particularly long time, and what has my relationship been to it over the years?

(For example, "I want to take a vacation by myself. I've wanted this for at least the last 10 years. I find it hard to justify doing so. I have a tendency to look up retreat centers online, but I or other people end up talking me out of going or something comes up that takes over my life.")

What are some of the deeper challenges, as well as secret hopes, I have around this desire?

(For example, "I learned at an early age that I should spend my spare time working hard, taking care of others, and being useful to my loved ones. I've always had difficulty enjoying unstructured time, because I worry that I should be productive and service-oriented. But some part of me understands that if I do this for myself, it could change my life and make me happier, less stressed, and more connected to myself."

Exercise

Your Shadow Desire

Commit to cultivating a relationship with the shadow desire you identified in the last prompt by coming up with three ways you'll honor it in the next week.

(For example, "I'll take myself out on a date. I'll block off an hour on Saturday to dance to my favorite music. I'll buy myself champagne and chocolate-covered strawberries, then take a bubble bath.")

Action 1:

Action 2:

Action 3:

Next commit to asking someone in your life to do something specific for you to help fulfill your shadow desire. Remember, even if they say no, you'll continue to honor your desire. You might also play with collaborating with the other person so you can both feel good about whatever you decide.

(For example, "I'll ask the person I'm dating to give me a candlelit massage. Come to think of it, it might be nice to give them a massage, too, so maybe I'll suggest we take turns. I'll ask them to share any challenges they might have around desire and pleasure, so we can feel closer and more connected.")

My ask:

MEDITATION

Meeting Desire

Use the QR code below to access a short meditation that will help you envision how it feels to be met in your desire. Maybe you've found it difficult to imagine a world where you get to be connected to your desire and where you can experience nourishment on a daily basis. This visualization will help you not only to feel more connected to your desire, but to experience it as a powerful energy that can bring you into a more meaningful relationship with other people and the world around you.

STAGE 7:
WHOLENESS

ALCHEMICAL STAGE—COAGULATION:

The process of a liquid turning into a solid state (such as blood turning into a scab when a wound heals).

In shadow work, this is the solidification of your authentic, whole self—free from binaries of good and bad. Your polarities have unified to reveal a totality more glorious than its separate parts. The gold of your true self has cooled and solidified to show you what's possible when you stay connected with your deeper essence.

✦ ✦ ✦

You have explored, embraced, and integrated your shadow, and you are stepping into your **Wholeness**. This is the stage at which all the scavenging in the darkness has led to a remarkable discovery: Inside the cave of your shadow lives your most radiant light. In fact, the quest to collect the pieces of you that were unwittingly left behind is the very thing that's made you shine so bright.

By now, you're reflecting a soft vulnerability and transparency that lights you up from within. By seeing yourself in this new light, you open up to greater possibility, thus empowering yourself and those around you. Wholeness isn't just the goal, though; it's the first step on a new journey through life, where you get to live in full ownership of both your shadow and light.

No matter where you are on your shadow work journey, you're always invited to step even more decisively into your luminosity. Because the deeper you travel into the darkness, the brighter you'll shine.

Stepping into Visibility

At this stage, you've already done the work of illuminating more and more of who you are. Like the full moon, you've gone through a series of phases, and now you're revealing what you once concealed. You're no longer stuck in the belief that you should hide any part of yourself. In fact, you've already experienced the fulfillment and satisfaction that are possible when you experience your true self instead of running from it.

Visibility isn't just about being seen by others; it's about consciously shining your light on yourself. The more you allow yourself to be truly visible, the more genuine and intimate your overall life will be.

You were probably taught that it's not okay to claim the aspects of yourself that are unique, beautiful, and worthy of applause and attention. You were probably trained to disown not just the qualities you view as negative, but the very ones that define your essential goodness.

So, how do you know if you're dimming your light and relegating yourself to invisibility? Below are some of the most common ways:

- Not voicing your opinion if you think it's going to be unpopular or invite conflict
- Deflecting or brushing off compliments

- Dismissing attention when it's rightfully placed on you
- Downplaying an accomplishment or gain
- Feeling fearful of intimidating someone else with your intelligence, beauty, confidence, etc.
- Hiding beneath excess weight or clothing, or other methods of concealing yourself

On the opposite end of the spectrum—deliberately making yourself larger than life so that others will notice and validate you.

The thing to remember about visibility is that it's less about who's looking at you and more about how you carry yourself—no matter how others might react. Most of us were taught to see ourselves reflected in the eyes of others. But when you inhabit genuine visibility, you no longer need to be reflected by someone else because you've become your own clear, radiant, self-evident source of light.

When you let yourself be visible, you become the agent of your own freedom. You're no longer passively waiting for someone else's validation or approval. Instead, you take up space and let yourself shine from the inside out, whether other people notice or not. But you'd best believe this courageous reclamation of your light is very likely to garner results and turn heads in the world around you!

From "Letting Myself Go" to "Letting Go"

There's a big misconception that's at play in our society. It sounds a little something like: *You can't expect to shine if you let yourself go.*

The idea of letting yourself go is connected to becoming careless, untidy, or uninhibited in ways that make you look bad. Again, this is dependent on how others might perceive you.

Wholeness is about liberation, so when you're at this stage of shadow work, you're transmuting "letting myself go" into "letting go." It's a totally different energy. Letting go isn't about feeling sorry for or bad about yourself; it's about liberating yourself from other people's judgments and expectations and even from the faulty perception that the world is busy judging you.

You're able to face reality with greater acceptance. Instead of tucking in your tummy, or refusing to let yourself be seen unless you have a full face of makeup, or avoiding contact with others when you've spiraled into the darkness of difficult thoughts, you connect with the possibility that who you are, as you are, is *enough.*

Many of us unconsciously consent to thinking and acting in ways that don't actually correspond to who we are deep down, because that's how we've learned to belong: to our family, our peer group, and our society. But instead of thinking, *There's something wrong with me, so I'll be or do what someone else wants*, start to recognize that manipulating something about yourself in order to belong isn't true belonging—it means you're crossing your boundaries to be in a situation or relationship that isn't worthy of you.

Shadow work helps you come back to your true nature and reinforces your aliveness. When you move through all seven stages, you're no longer invested in suffering, hiding, or doing things in order to be perceived a certain way. You rightly conclude that it's easier to be with what is instead of piling on more armor.

When you let go of any external references about your worth, beauty, lovability, and overall acceptability, it becomes easier to be with what *is*. You start to fill up from the inside out rather than the outside in. And it's your genuine essence, which shines out from every cell, that has the power to magnetize the right people and situations.

Every single one of us is a work in progress, and the invitation is to hold the paradox: You can accept yourself 100 percent as you are, even as you're in the continuous process of becoming. When you align with your deepest truth, you step onto the continuous path of evolution and growth. You might make it out of the caterpillar phase, but you get to be a butterfly more than once.

JOURNAL PROMPTS

Wholeness

Integrating the Alchemical Process

You've been through a lot on this journey to transforming the raw materials of your shadow into the gold of your wholeness. Take some time to reflect on the impact of each stage of this journey. Without thinking too hard, write about what each stage represents to you.

My awareness has helped me to see:

Surrender lets me accept:

I am claiming responsibility for:

My authenticity feels like:

My resilience allows me to commit to:

When I follow nourishment by claiming my desires, I experience:

Embracing Wholeness

When I embrace my wholeness, not what anyone else wants me to be, I feel (you may wish to define how wholeness feels in your body so you can anchor the sensation within):

Here are some memories, experiences, dreams, symbols, stories, etc., that tangibly connect me to my wholeness (use all your senses here, including colors, textures, sounds, etc.):

Here's how I'm committing to visibility and letting go so I can shine even more brightly:

Voyaging through the Shadow

Here's what shadow work is teaching me about myself:

These are some of the remaining questions I have:

I'd like freedom from:

I'd like freedom to be, do, or have:

Here are the parts of myself I intend to continue exploring with shadow work:

Exercise

Meeting Your Gaze

During the responsibility stage, on page 76, you completed the exercise titled I Am That, where you gazed into the mirror and claimed a disowned shadow quality. One powerful way to remove the painful sting of self-judgment is to balance raw honesty with positive, self-loving mirror work.

You deserve to meet your own gaze from a place of love and tenderness. For this exercise, meet your reflection for five whole minutes without looking away or trying to fix anything. Instead, see yourself, feel yourself, and love yourself. Louise Hay, the founder of Hay House, never passed a reflective surface without showering herself with affirmations and compliments. Notice how it feels to stand only in positive self-regard. Bathe in your light. Let yourself soften and receive the gift of your wholeness.

When I met my own gaze in the mirror, here's what happened (note any emotions, sensations, thoughts, and surprises):

MEDITATION

Shining Your Light

Use the QR code below to access a short meditation that will guide you to fill up with your full essence and to notice how it impacts you and the world. When you explore your darkest shadow, you find your brightest light. In this guided visualization, you'll emanate a field of radiance from the inside out so you can confidently step into any situation with the awareness that you're much bigger than your mind or body: You're a force of nature. And when you shine your wholeness, you give others permission to do the same.

Your Personal Philosopher's Stone

Congratulations for making it through this journal! Please remember that shadow work is never done. We simply find new ways to enter the shadow's cave, uncover our wholeness, and radiate our light from the inside out. Now that you're here, it doesn't mean you won't ever go back into the cave or that there isn't plenty of stuff in the depths to unearth and bring to the surface. It just means that now that you've found a way in and no longer fear what you might find, you can replace fear or hesitation with curiosity and the spirit of exploration.

Shadow work is the most powerful thing you can choose to do on your journey of personal growth. You've been through the full cycle of the alchemical process to mine your inner gold and transmute the darkness of the unconscious into the light of understanding. Even if you don't immediately feel it, this process has already transformed you!

The continuous work of integrating your shadow solidifies your relationship with yourself and helps foster intimacy and connection with others and the world around you. When you're true to *you*—choosing to claim and love the parts you once muted or locked up to gain acceptance—you're free to dream up new possibilities that will fill up your life with greater meaning and purpose.

To that end, don't just close this journal and tuck it away. Because now that you've bravely gone where many choose not to venture, so much more is possible!

In Plato's *The Apology of Socrates*, Socrates famously said, "The unexamined life is not worth living," which could very well be the greatest endorsement of shadow work that's out there. Let this journal be an open invitation for you to bring your attention inward so you can fully know yourself and step into the multidimensional beauty of your life. Now that you have a compass and a way into the cave, may you continue to embrace your shadow to find your light.

Shining a Light on Your Shadow: An Ongoing Practice

Here's a simple shadow work process you can do anytime you feel troubled or activated. When this happens, the tendency is to point a finger and blame someone else, which keeps you more disconnected from your shadow and more prone to disown specific qualities. Instead, commit to exploring what's happening inside you and to reclaiming a shadow quality you haven't yet integrated. The first two pages offer an example of insights that can be excavated.

The situation that's provoking me now
and making me want to explore my shadow:

Whenever I talk to my friend, she always goes on and on about herself and doesn't ask me what's going on in my life. It's hard for me to get a word in.

Awareness

The shadow quality I discovered is:
Selfishness

The judgments I have about this quality are:
Selfish people disregard the needs of others.
Selfish people take up a lot of space.

Surrender

I resist this shadow quality in myself by:
People-pleasing and over-giving.

I accept that this quality shows up in me when:
I say no to something I don't want to do.

Responsibility

When it comes to the ways I've displayed this shadow quality, I still need to forgive myself for:
The time when I took a solo vacation instead of going home for the holidays.

The gift of this shadow quality that I'm reclaiming is:
The ability to honor my own needs.

Authenticity

Here's how I'm holding back my truth in this situation:
I shrink and go silent when I talk to my friend.

I can call on this shadow quality for support and guidance in expressing my truth by:
The next time we talk, initiating the conversation around what I have going on instead of deferring to listening.

Resilience

The shadow commitment I've been upholding around this situation is:
Not rocking the boat of our friendship.

The new commitment I'm making to align with my authenticity is:
Taking up space and holding space.

Nourishment

In this situation, I've been depriving myself of:
Support from my friend.

A desire I have that I can meet is:
I can be protective of my time and how much of it I spend with this friend.

Wholeness

I give myself permission to release:
Needing to be liked and needing to keep the peace.

I give myself permission to embrace:
Doing what serves me best.

✦ ✦ ✦

The situation that's provoking me now
and making me want to explore my shadow:

Awareness

The shadow quality I discovered is:

The judgments I have about this quality are:

Surrender

I resist this shadow quality by:

I accept that this quality shows up in me when:

Responsibility

When it comes to this shadow quality, I still need to forgive myself for:

The gift of this shadow quality that I'm reclaiming is:

Authenticity

Here's how I'm holding back my truth:

I can call on this shadow quality for support and guidance in expressing my truth by:

Resilience

The shadow commitment I've been upholding around this situation is:

The new commitment I'm making to align with my authenticity is:

Nourishment

In this situation, I've been depriving myself of:

A desire I have that I can meet is:

Wholeness

I give myself permission to release:

I give myself permission to embrace:

✦ ✦ ✦

The situation that's provoking me now
and making me want to explore my shadow:

Awareness

The shadow quality I discovered is:

The judgments I have about this quality are:

Surrender

I resist this shadow quality by:

I accept that this quality shows up in me when:

Responsibility

When it comes to this shadow quality, I still need to forgive myself for:

The gift of this shadow quality that I'm reclaiming is:

Authenticity

Here's how I'm holding back my truth:

I can call on this shadow quality for support and guidance in expressing my truth by:

Resilience

The shadow commitment I've been upholding around this situation is:

The new commitment I'm making to align with my authenticity is:

Nourishment

In this situation, I've been depriving myself of:

A desire I have that I can meet is:

Wholeness

I give myself permission to release:

I give myself permission to embrace:

✦ ✦ ✦

The situation that's provoking me now
and making me want to explore my shadow:

Awareness

The shadow quality I discovered is:

The judgments I have about this quality are:

Surrender

I resist this shadow quality by:

I accept that this quality shows up in me when:

Responsibility

When it comes to this shadow quality, I still need to forgive myself for:

The gift of this shadow quality that I'm reclaiming is:

Authenticity

Here's how I'm holding back my truth:

I can call on this shadow quality for support and guidance in expressing my truth by:

Resilience

The shadow commitment I've been upholding around this situation is:

The new commitment I'm making to align with my authenticity is:

Nourishment

In this situation, I've been depriving myself of:

A desire I have that I can meet is:

Wholeness

I give myself permission to release:

I give myself permission to embrace:

✦ ✦ ✦

The situation that's provoking me now
and making me want to explore my shadow:

Awareness

The shadow quality I discovered is:

The judgments I have about this quality are:

Surrender

I resist this shadow quality by:

I accept that this quality shows up in me when:

Responsibility

*When it comes to this shadow quality, I still need to forgive
myself for:*

The gift of this shadow quality that I'm reclaiming is:

Authenticity

Here's how I'm holding back my truth:

I can call on this shadow quality for support and guidance in expressing my truth by:

Resilience

The shadow commitment I've been upholding around this situation is:

The new commitment I'm making to align with my authenticity is:

Nourishment

In this situation, I've been depriving myself of:

A desire I have that I can meet is:

Wholeness

I give myself permission to release:

I give myself permission to embrace:

✦ ✦ ✦

The situation that's provoking me now
and making me want to explore my shadow:

Awareness

The shadow quality I discovered is:

The judgments I have about this quality are:

Surrender

I resist this shadow quality by:

I accept that this quality shows up in me when:

Responsibility

When it comes to this shadow quality, I still need to forgive myself for:

The gift of this shadow quality that I'm reclaiming is:

Authenticity

Here's how I'm holding back my truth:

I can call on this shadow quality for support and guidance in expressing my truth by:

Resilience

The shadow commitment I've been upholding around this situation is:

The new commitment I'm making to align with my authenticity is:

Nourishment

In this situation, I've been depriving myself of:

A desire I have that I can meet is:

Wholeness

I give myself permission to release:

I give myself permission to embrace:

✦ ✦ ✦

The situation that's provoking me now
and making me want to explore my shadow:

Awareness

The shadow quality I discovered is:

The judgments I have about this quality are:

Surrender

I resist this shadow quality by:

I accept that this quality shows up in me when:

Responsibility

When it comes to this shadow quality, I still need to forgive myself for:

The gift of this shadow quality that I'm reclaiming is:

Authenticity

Here's how I'm holding back my truth:

I can call on this shadow quality for support and guidance in expressing my truth by:

Resilience

The shadow commitment I've been upholding around this situation is:

The new commitment I'm making to align with my authenticity is:

Nourishment

In this situation, I've been depriving myself of:

A desire I have that I can meet is:

Wholeness

I give myself permission to release:

I give myself permission to embrace:

✦ ✦ ✦

About the Author

NANCY LEVIN, certified master coach, author of several books, podcast host, and founder of Levin Life Coach Academy, is an expert in shadow work, exploring your unconscious mind to uncover the parts of yourself that you've repressed and hidden. Nancy was trained and mentored by Debbie Ford who is credited with bringing the concept of shadow work to a mass audience through her appearances on *The Oprah Winfrey Show* and *Super Soul Sunday.* The best-selling author of many books, including *The Dark Side of the Light Chasers,* Debbie was an internationally recognized transformational coach, speaker, and teacher for more than 20 years. Nancy was personally selected by Debbie to carry on her legacy.

Visit her online at **nancylevin.com.**

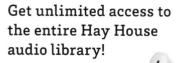

Hay House Titles of Related Interest

YOU CAN HEAL YOUR LIFE, the movie,
starring Louise Hay & Friends
(available as an online streaming video)
www.hayhouse.com/louise-movie

THE SHIFT, the movie,
starring Dr. Wayne W. Dyer
(available as an online streaming video)
www.hayhouse.com/the-shift-movie

✦ ✦ ✦

*THE ART OF CHANGE, A GUIDED JOURNAL: 8 Weeks to Making
a Meaningful Shift in Your Life,* by Nancy Levin

*THE GIFT OF GRATITUDE: A Guided Journal for Counting Your
Blessings,* by Louise Hay

*LIVING YOUR PURPOSE JOURNAL: A Guided Path to Finding
Success and Inner Peace,* by Dr. Wayne W. Dyer

THE COSMIC JOURNAL, by Yanik Silver

THE HIGH 5 DAILY JOURNAL, by Mel Robbins

All of the above are available at your local bookstore,
or may be ordered by contacting Hay House (see next page).

✦ ✦ ✦